Companion to the
Revised Common Lectionary

5. Before We Worship

Already published

Companion to the Revised Common Lectionary

Norman Wallwork

Companion to the Revised Common Lectionary

5. Before We Worship

A New Collection of
Vestry Prayers

EPWORTH PRESS

British Library Cataloguing in Publication data

A catalogue record of this book is available
from the British Library

0 7162 0547 5

First published 2001 by
Epworth Press
20 Ivatt Way
Peterborough, PE3 7PG

Typeset by Regent Typesetting
Printed and bound by
Biddles Ltd, Guildford and King's Lynn

In thankfulness
for the lives of

PHILIP BLACKBURN
RAYMOND GEORGE
GORDON WAKEFIELD
and
NEVILLE WARD

men of prayer
and catholic love

Contents

Preface

Now in its fifth impression, *A Book of Vestry Prayers* has been in print continuously for twenty-five years. However, there are several reasons why an entirely new book is called for. Since the first edition in 1976 liturgical language has moved entirely into modern English. The 'thou form' has been abandoned. Also, twenty-five years ago many English churches were using the calendar and lectionary of the Joint Liturgical Group. Present-day calendars and lessons are now, for the most part, based on the Revised Common Lectionary.

In our vestries some of the best prayers said with those who officiate at worship are extempore, without a book. So are some of the worst! This new collection offers material carefully selected or written to help those who appreciate short and appropriate printed prayers.

Since the first edition of *A Book of Vestry Prayers* many more collects have appeared in the service books and prayer anthologies published throughout the English-speaking world and a number of these are included in this new book.

I still recall the encouragement of my tutors Geoffrey Wainwright and W. Jardine Grisbrooke when the first edition of *A Book of Vestry Prayers* was being prepared and now I am grateful to the Revd Gerald Burt and the members of the Editorial Committee of the Epworth Press for encouraging me to compile a new edition.

Norman Wallwork
Michaelmas, 2000

Introduction

The busy minutes which precede an act of worship are precious. They can either contribute to the service or detract from it. To ensure that these prayers bring the greatest possible blessing, the following points should be noted.

- The appropriate prayer should be chosen well in advance and read through before it is used. This will ensure that its meaning is clear both to the one who reads it and to those who will listen. This method also enables the prayer to come from the heart.
- On the major Holy Days,* only the appropriate prayers are said, even if there is a baptism or confirmation.
- Church diaries, preaching plans and the religious press usually indicate the appropriate titles for each Sunday. A regular check will avoid confusion.
- Ideally there are five stages to each prayer:

  1. The bidding 'Let us pray'
  2. A short silence
  3. The Prayer
  4. The Amen
  5. Another short silence

* Christmas Day, Good Friday, Easter Day, Ascension Day, Whit Sunday, Trinity Sunday and All Saints' Day.

Part One

Prayers for the Church's Year

First Sunday of Advent

Gracious God,
as the day of our redemption draws near,
extend to us your saving mercy,
that our lives may be filled with your grace
and our worship may show forth your praise;
through Jesus Christ our Lord. **Amen.**

C. N. R. Wallwork

God our deliverer,
whose approaching birth still shakes the foundations of our world,
may we so wait for your coming with eagerness and hope
that we embrace without terror the labour pangs of the new age;
through Jesus Christ our Lord. **Amen.**

Janet Morley, *All Desires Known*

Second Sunday of Advent

Lord our God,
since you will return to us in judgment
in an hour that we least expect,
grant us to watch and pray at all times,
so that whether you come in the evening, or at midnight, or in the
    morning,
your people may be found among those who are waiting and watching
for the advent of their Redeemer;
to whom be all glory and praise, now and for ever. **Amen.**

Non-jurors' Prayer Book, 1734

Gracious Father,
by whose tender compassion the light of Christ has dawned upon us:
open our hearts, so that joyfully receiving Christ,
we may declare his glory to the ends of the earth;
who lives and reigns with you and the Holy Spirit,
one God, for ever and ever. **Amen.**

Uniting in Worship, 1988

Third Sunday of Advent

God of glory and compassion,
at your touch the wilderness blossoms,
broken lives are made whole,
and fearful hearts grow strong in faith.
Open our eyes to your presence
and waken our hearts to sing your praise.
To all who long for the coming of your Son
grant patience and perseverance,
that we may announce in word and deed
the good news of your kingdom.
We ask this through him whose coming is certain,
and whose day draws near:
your Son, our Lord Jesus Christ. **Amen.**

ICEL Collects, 1997

By your power, Sovereign Lord,
John the Baptist was born into the world
as forerunner of the promised Messiah:
Help us to heed his message
of repentance and amendment of life,
and to follow his example of boldness and self-denial;
through Jesus Christ our Lord. **Amen.**

Collects with the New Lectionary, 1973

Fourth Sunday of Advent

Almighty and everlasting God,
the Light of the faithful
and the Ruler of souls:
you make us holy by the incarnation of your Word,
and by the child-bearing of the Blessed Virgin Mary:
let the power of your Holy Spirit come also upon us,
and the mercy of the Most High overshadow us;
through Jesus Christ our Saviour and Redeemer. **Amen.**

Mozarabic Missal

Almighty God,
Mary gave birth to a Son
who offers salvation to the whole world.
May we, like Mary,
both treasure him in our hearts
and bring him to others;
through the same Christ our Lord. **Amen.**

A Christian's Prayer Book, 1973

Christmas Eve (Early Evening)

God our Father,
whose Word comes among us,
in the Holy Child of Bethlehem:
let the light of faith illumine our hearts,
and shine in our words and deeds;
through Christ our Lord,
who lives and reigns with you and the Holy Spirit,
one God, now and for ever. **Amen.**

Uniting in Worship, 1988

Eternal Father,
we give you thanks for your incarnate Son,
whose name is our salvation.
Plant in every heart, we pray,
the love of our Lord and Saviour, Jesus Christ,
who lives and reigns with you and the Holy Spirit,
one God, in glory everlasting. **Amen.**

Common Order, 1994

Christmas (Midnight)

O God,
you have hallowed this sacred night
with the joyful tidings of the Word made flesh:
Grant us so to venerate the mystery of Christ's glory upon earth,
that we may at the last behold him face to face,
in the fullness of his eternal majesty in heaven;
this we ask for his sake. **Amen.**

C. N. R. Wallwork

Lord Jesus Christ,
Child of Bethlehem and Son of God:
help us this night
to join our songs of glory
with those of the heavenly host,
that the joy of the church on earth
may be heard in the praise of heaven;
this we ask for your name's sake. **Amen.**

C. N. R. Wallwork

Christmas Day (During the Day)

Grant, O Lord our God,
that we who rejoice to keep the feast
of the Nativity of Jesus Christ our Lord,
may by walking worthily of him
attain to fellowship with him;
through the same Christ our Lord. **Amen.**

Leonine Sacramentary

Today, O Lord,
you have gathered into one,
things earthly and heavenly,
through the gift of your beloved Son,
our new-born brother.
As we continue our earthly pilgrimage,
may your light shine in our hearts,
and may we see the glory of Christ,
born in our midst;
this we ask for his sake. **Amen.**

A Christian's Prayer Book, 1973

The First Sunday of Christmas*

(The Sunday between 26 December and 31 December inclusive)

* (If 6 January is a weekday, the previous Sunday is observed as 'The Sunday of the Epiphany', see page 12)

O God,
you cradle us at the beginning of life
and embrace us at our journey's end,
for you love us as your own.
Bind our family life together
and deepen our faith,
that, like the Holy Family,
we may grow in wisdom,
obedient to your word.
We ask this through Jesus Christ, your Word made flesh,
who lives and reigns with you in the unity of the Holy Spirit,
God for ever and ever. **Amen.**

ICEL Collects, 1997

Almighty God,
you have shed upon us the new light
of your incarnate Word.
May this light, enkindled in our hearts,
shine forth in our lives;
through Jesus Christ our Lord. **Amen**

Book of Alternative Services of the Anglican Church of Canada, 1985

The Second Sunday of Christmas*

(The Sunday between 1 and 5 January inclusive)

** (If 6 January is a weekday, the previous Sunday is observed as
'The Sunday of the Epiphany', see page 12)*

We thank you, Lord our God,
for the gift of your Son
whom you commanded to be called Jesus;
grant that we may so honour his name on earth,
that others may be led to him who alone is Lord and Saviour,
now and for ever. **Amen.**

A New Zealand Prayer Book, 1989

God eternal,
from your tender mercy
your Word has sprung forth,
taking our flesh in the womb of Mary.
Breathe forth your Spirit upon us
that we may proclaim the message of this Holy Child
all the days of our life;
through Jesus Christ our hope and our Redeemer. **Amen.**

Prayers for Dawn and Dusk, 1992

The Epiphany of the Lord (6 January)

or, The Sunday of the Epiphany
(i.e. The Sunday before 6 January)

O Lord God,
who gave to wise men of old
a glorious star to lead them to the Christ:
grant that we to whom you have given a yet more glorious sign,
even his holy Cross,
may follow and be led by it the whole way
to our salvation and your heaven;
through the same Christ our Lord. **Amen.**

Eric Milner-White

O God our Father,
who by the shining of a star
led the wise men to the city of David:
guide us by the light of your Spirit,
that we too may come into the presence of Jesus
and offer our gifts and our worship to him,
our Saviour and our Lord. **Amen.**

Alan Warren

The Sunday of the Baptism of the Lord

'The First Sunday in Ordinary Time' (The First Sunday after the Epiphany i.e. The Sunday between 7 and 13 January inclusive)

Heavenly Father,
by the power of your Holy Spirit
you give to your faithful people new life
in the waters of baptism.
Guide and strengthen us by the same Spirit,
that we who are born again
may serve you in faith and love,
and grow into the full stature of your Son, Jesus Christ our Lord.
   Amen.

Common Worship: Initiation Services, 1998

Father,
when Jesus was baptized in the Jordan,
you proclaimed him as your well-beloved Son,
and the Holy Spirit came upon him.
May your Spirit guide and help us
to share in your ministry to others;
through the same Jesus Christ our Lord. **Amen.**

A Christian's Prayer Book, 1973

The Sunday between 14 and 20 January inclusive

'The Second Sunday in Ordinary Time' (The Second Sunday after the Epiphany)

Almighty God,
your Son our Saviour Jesus Christ is the light of the world.
May your people,
illumined by your word and sacraments,
shine with the radiance of his glory,
that he may be known, worshipped and obeyed
to the ends of the earth;
who lives and reigns with you and the Holy Spirit,
one God, now and for ever. **Amen.**

Book of Common Prayer of the Episcopal Church, 1977

Lord and heavenly Father,
in this hour of worship,
let us be mindful of your presence,
that we may draw near to you
with reverent and humble hearts,
and offer prayers and praise
acceptable in your sight;
through Jesus Christ our Lord. **Amen.**

Frank Colquhoun, 1982

The Sunday between 21 and 27 January inclusive

'The Third Sunday in Ordinary Time' (The Third Sunday after the Epiphany)

God of all mercy,
your Son brought good news to the despairing,
freedom to the oppressed
and joy to the sad;
fill us with your Spirit,
that the people of our day may see in us his likeness
and glorify your name;
through Christ our Lord. **Amen.**

A New Zealand Prayer Book, 1989

Lord Jesus Christ,
you called your disciples
to proclaim your kingdom,
and to teach your commandments:
give to your disciples this day
such an understanding of your word,
that we may teach others what we have been taught by you;
through Jesus Christ our Lord. **Amen.**

Daily Prayer

The Sunday between 28 January and 3 February inclusive*

'The Fourth Sunday in Ordinary Time'
(The Fourth Sunday after the Epiphany)

* (Unless it is 'The Sunday before Lent')

Almighty God,
our heavenly Father,
whose Son Jesus Christ came to cast fire on the earth;
grant that by the prayers of your faithful people
a fire of burning zeal may be kindled,
and pass from heart to heart,
till all our hardness is melted
in the warmth of your love;
through him who loved us
and gave himself for us,
Jesus Christ our Lord. **Amen.**

G. C. Binyon

Look upon us, O Lord,
and let the darkness of our souls vanish
before the beams of your brightness.
Fill us with holy love,
and open to us the treasures of your wisdom.
As we seek your face, show us your glory,
that our longing may be satisfied
and our peace be perfect;
through Jesus Christ our Lord. **Amen.**

Adapted from a prayer of Saint Augustine

The Presentation of Christ in the Temple (Candlemas)*
2 February

*(Candlemas may be celebrated on the nearest Sunday,
but not on 'The Sunday before Lent')*

Inspired by your Spirit, Lord,
we gather in your house to welcome your Son.
Enlighten our minds
and lay bare our thoughts.
Purify us,
and make us obedient to your law,
that we may mature in wisdom
and grow into the full stature of your grace;
through Jesus Christ our Lord;
who lives and reigns with you,
and the Holy Spirit, one God, now and for ever. **Amen.**

ICEL Collects, 1997

God of our salvation,
as Mary and Joseph offered
your only-begotten Son in the Temple,
so may we offer ourselves to you.
Receive our sacrifice of praise
and assist us to proclaim your goodness throughout the world;
for the sake of the same Christ our Lord. **Amen.**

Pray Without Ceasing, 1993 adapted

The Sunday between 4 and 10 February inclusive*

'The Fifth Sunday in Ordinary Time'
(The Fifth Sunday after the Epiphany)

* (Unless it is 'The Sunday before Lent' or falls in Lent)

Fill us, O Lord, with your Holy Spirit
that we may see all heaven before our eyes,
rejoice in the glory of your kingdom
and set forth in our praise
the wonders of your redeeming love;
and this we ask through Christ our Lord. **Amen**

Jacob Boehme

Lord Jesus Christ,
Word of God,
Saviour of the world
and King of saints;
accept the worship of your church
and through its ministry
speak to us,
save us,
and bring us to eternal life;
for your name's sake. **Amen.**

C. N. R. Wallwork

The Sunday between 11 and 17 February inclusive*

'The Sixth Sunday in Ordinary Time'
(The Sixth Sunday after the Epiphany)

* (Unless it is 'The Sunday before Lent' or falls in Lent)

Almighty God,
you have given a day of rest
to your people,
and, through your Spirit in the church,
you have consecrated the first day of the week
to be a perpetual memorial
of your Son's resurrection:
grant that we may so use your gift
that, refreshed and strengthened in soul and body,
we may serve you faithfully
all the days of our life;
through the same Christ our Lord. **Amen.**

The Book of Worship

Eternal God and Father,
in whose presence we find rest and peace:
as we come to you now,
may we be cleansed and strengthened
by your Holy Spirit,
and serve you with a quiet mind;
through Christ our Lord. **Amen.**

New Every Morning

The Sunday between 18 and 24 February*

'The Seventh Sunday in Ordinary Time' (The Seventh Sunday after Epiphany)

* *(Unless it is 'The Sunday before Lent' or falls in Lent)*

God of mercy,
be swift to help us,
as our lips pour forth your praise;
and fill our lives with your peace,
as we open our hearts to your word
and wait for your salvation;
through Jesus Christ our Lord. **Amen.**

Michael Perham, *Celebrating Common Prayer*, 1992, altered

Eternal God,
grant that by your grace
our speaking and hearing
may be to your praise,
to the glory of your kingdom,
and for our peace and salvation;
through Jesus Christ our Lord. **Amen.**

*Service Book and Ordinal of the
Presbyterian Church of South Africa*, 1969

The Sunday between 25 and 29 February inclusive*

'The Eighth Sunday in Ordinary Time'
(The Eighth Sunday after the Epiphany)

* (Unless it is 'The Sunday before Lent' or falls in Lent)

Lord our God,
perpetually present with your people;
through the gift of your Spirit,
bless us by the ministry of your Word,
that we be enlightened, refreshed and strengthened
for the work that you have given us to do.
This we ask, for the sake of your Son our Saviour, Jesus Christ.
Amen.

C. N. R. Wallwork

Gracious God,
help us in this act of worship,
to seek above all things
your kingdom of righteousness and peace;
that we may receive at your hands
every good and perfect gift
which a loving Father bestows upon his children;
through Christ our Lord. **Amen.**

C. N. R. Wallwork

The Sunday before Lent
(The Sunday of the Transfiguration)

Spirit of the Most High,
overshadow us with the brightness of your glory,
and speak to us out of the cloud of your presence;
that as by faith we see Jesus
wearing the robe of our nature,
made white and radiant,
we may hear the Father's voice:
'This is my beloved Son, my chosen, listen to him.'
We make our prayer through the same Christ our Lord,
who lives and reigns with the Father and with you, O Holy Spirit,
one God, now and for ever. **Amen.**

James Ferguson

Open our eyes, O God, to your glory,
that we may worship you in spirit and in truth,
and offer to you
the praise of glad and thankful hearts;
through Christ our Lord. **Amen.**

New Every Morning, 1973

Ash Wednesday
(The First Day of Lent)

God of compassion,
through your Son Jesus Christ
you have reconciled your people to yourself.
As we follow his example of prayer and fasting,
may we obey you with willing hearts
and serve one another in holy love;
through Jesus Christ our Lord. **Amen**

Book of Alternative Services of the
Anglican Church of Canada, 1985

God our Father
give to us contrite hearts;
and through Christ,
who bore our sins in his body on the tree,
heal our wounds.
By your Holy Spirit,
who leads us into all truth,
speak to us your pardon and peace;
and this we ask for your mercy's sake. **Amen.**

Michael Perham, *Enriching the Christian Year*, 1993, altered

The First Sunday in Lent

Grant, O Lord,
that throughout this season of Lent,
we may enter more deeply into the mystery of Christ,
and draw upon its power
all the days of our life;
through Jesus Christ our Lord. **Amen.**

Sunday Celebration of the Word and Hours, 1995, altered

Gracious God,
only when you turn your face towards us
do we find salvation.
By the power of your Spirit
may our prayer and fasting
draw us to the heart of the gospel
and deepen our faith in a crucified God;
this we ask through Christ our Lord. **Amen.**

C. N. R. Wallwork

The Second Sunday in Lent

Grant to your people, O Lord,
the gift of your Spirit,
that we may learn to profess our faith with courage
and announce with joy the wonder of your love.
We ask this through our Lord Jesus Christ,
who lives and reigns with you
in the unity of the Holy Spirit,
one God, for ever and ever. **Amen.**

Messale Romano, 1983

Eternal Light,
shed the beams of your mercy upon us,
and instruct us by your word,
that we may know your will
and rejoice in your salvation;
through Jesus Christ our Lord. **Amen**

Book of Common Order, 1940, altered

The Third Sunday in Lent

Lord our God,
by your Holy Spirit
write your commandments upon our hearts
and grant us the wisdom and power of the Cross;
so that, cleansed from all greed and self-seeking,
we may become a living temple of your love;
through Jesus Christ our Lord. **Amen.**

A Prayer Book for Australia, 1995

Lord of all power and might,
assist the praises of your people,
that we may worthily celebrate
the mystery of your love
and the triumphs of your grace;
through Jesus Christ our Lord. **Amen.**

C. N. R. Wallwork

The Fourth Sunday in Lent (Mothering Sunday)

God our Father,
you look for the return of your wandering children,
and lovingly embrace them when they come back to you.
Therefore with confidence we approach your throne
that we may receive mercy,
and find grace to help in time of need;
through Christ our Lord. **Amen.**

Lent, Holy Week and Easter, 1984

Loving God,
like a mother you give life and breath
to your children.
May your church which looks to you in its need
be nourished for ever by the passion of your Son,
our Saviour, Jesus Christ. **Amen.**

C. N. R. Wallwork

The Fifth Sunday in Lent
(The First Sunday of the Passion)

Help us, O Lord,
to show how sweet it is to love you,
to bear with you,
to weep with you,
and for ever to rejoice with you;
through Christ our Lord. **Amen.**

Unknown, sometimes attributed to Melanchthon

Lord Jesus Christ,
draw near to your people
from the throne of your heavenly glory;
that as we contemplate your bitter pain
upon the holy Cross,
we may be strengthened
by the proclamation of its life-giving mystery;
for your mercy and your truth's sake. **Amen.**

C. N. R. Wallwork

The Sixth Sunday in Lent
(The Second Sunday of the Passion)
'Palm Sunday'

Lord Jesus Christ,
who on this day entered the rebellious city
where you were to die,
and there received the blessings of your disciples:
make us ready to lay our tributes at your feet
and to greet you as the One who comes in the name of the Lord.
And grant that having confessed and worshipped you on earth,
we may be among those who will greet you in the glory of heaven;
where you reign for ever and ever. **Amen.**

Book of Common Order, 1940, adapted

Lord Jesus Christ,
accept our songs of praise
as you journey to your Cross;
and enable us both to grieve at its necessity
and to be renewed by its power;
for your own name's sake. **Amen.**

C. N. R. Wallwork

Monday, Tuesday and Wednesday of Holy Week

God our Father,
you have revealed your glory
in the life and words of your Son, our Saviour.
Help us to receive his teaching,
and to bring to his feet
the fragrance and beauty of our praise and love;
and this we ask for his sake. **Amen.**

A New Zealand Prayer Book, 1989, altered

O God,
by the passion of your blessed Son,
you made an instrument of shameful death
to be for us the means of life.
May our lives be so transformed by his passion
that we may witness to his grace;
who lives and reigns with you and the Holy Spirit,
one God, now and for ever. **Amen.**

*The Book of Alternative Services of the
Anglican Church of Canada*, 1985

Maundy Thursday

O God,
by the example of your Son, our Saviour Jesus Christ,
you taught us the greatness of true humility,
and call us to watch with him in his passion.
Give us grace to serve one another in lowliness,
and to enter into the fellowship of Christ's suffering;
in his name and for his sake. **Amen**

W. E. Orchard, *Divine Service*, 1919

Most merciful Redeemer,
in the celebration of your memorial supper
you have bequeathed to your church
the eucharistic feast of your eternal sacrifice.
Grant us faith to receive the grace
which you provide in this sacrament,
that we may eat at your royal banquet in heaven;
where you live and reign in glory,
with the Father and the Holy Spirit,
one God, now and for ever. **Amen.**

C. N. R. Wallwork

Good Friday

God of infinite love,
on this day of our salvation,
accept our gratitude for the words Christ uttered from the Cross,
accept our praise for the anguish he endured,
accept our worship for the sacrifice he offered
and accept our adoration for the victory he won;
this we ask for his sake. **Amen.**

Frank Colquhoun, *New Parish Prayers*, 1982, adapted

O God,
our salvation and truth,
grant that we your children,
rejecting the proud wisdom of this world,
may take up our place at the Cross of your dear Son.
May we walk in its way,
repose in its shadow,
venerate its mercy
and embrace its scorn;
through the same Christ our Lord. **Amen.**

Eric Milner-White

Easter Eve (Holy Saturday)

O God,
creator of heaven and earth,
as the crucified body of your dear Son was laid in the tomb
and rested on this holy Sabbath,
so may we await with him
the coming of the third day
and rise with him to newness of life;
who now lives and reigns with you and the Holy Spirit,
one God, now and for ever. **Amen.**

The Book of Common Prayer:
The Episcopal Church USA, 1977

O God,
your blessed Son
was laid in a tomb in a garden,
and rested on the Sabbath day:
Grant that we who have been buried with him
in the waters of baptism
may find our perfect rest
in his eternal and glorious kingdom;
where he lives and reigns for ever and ever. **Amen.**

The Book of Occasional Services, 1994

Easter Vigil

Lord God,
you have lit this night
with the radiance of the risen Christ;
may we who have been raised with him in baptism
reflect the light of his glory,
and live with him for ever. **Amen.**

A New Zealand Prayer Book, 1989

God of life,
through Jesus Christ
you have bestowed upon the world
the light of life.
As we celebrate the Passover of our Redeemer
may we share in his victory over death;
who lives and reigns
with you and the Holy Spirit,
now and for ever. **Amen.**

The United Methodist Book of Worship, 1992

Easter Day
(The First Sunday of Easter)

Risen Lord Jesus,
as Mary of Magdala met you in the garden
on the morning of your resurrection,
so may we meet you today.
Speak to us as you spoke to her
and reveal yourself as the living Lord.
Renew our hope,
kindle our joy
and send us out boldly proclaiming our Easter faith;
through Christ our Lord. **Amen.**

Frank Colquhoun, *Contemporary Parish Prayers*, 1975

Eternal God and Father,
by whose power our Lord Jesus Christ was raised from the dead;
with the whole company of the redeemed
we rejoice that he who was dead
is alive for evermore.
All glory, praise and thanksgiving,
all worship, honour and love,
be yours, almighty and everlasting God,
for ever and ever. **Amen.**

James M. Todd

The Second Sunday of Easter

God our Father,
through your only-begotten Son
you have overcome death,
and opened to us the gate of everlasting life;
grant that we who have been redeemed by his passion
may rejoice in his resurrection;
through the same Christ our Lord. **Amen.**

Gelasian Sacramentary

Be present, O Risen Lord,
in your church's Easter praise;
that its anthems of joy
and its proclamation of your victory
may worthily celebrate
both the mystery of your redeeming love
and the majesty of your eternal glory;
now and for ever. **Amen.**

C. N. R. Wallwork

The Third Sunday of Easter

Heavenly Father,
we give you thanks
that you have delivered us from the power of darkness
and brought us into the kingdom of your Son:
grant, that as by his death he has recalled us to life,
so by his continual presence in us
he may raise us to eternal joy;
for he lives and reigns with you, and the Holy Spirit,
now and for ever. **Amen.**

Mozarabic Missal

Lord Jesus Christ, our risen Saviour,
we give you thanks for your victory over sin and death;
we rejoice in your presence with us now,
and we worship you as the true and living One,
for you are alive for evermore;
and you reign with the Father
in the unity of the Holy Spirit,
one God for ever and ever. **Amen.**

C. N. R. Wallwork

The Fourth Sunday of Easter

O God,
whose Son Jesus Christ
is the Good Shepherd of his people:
grant that we may hear his voice,
know him when calls us by name
and follow him where he leads us;
who, with you and the Holy Spirit,
lives and reigns, one God,
for ever and ever. **Amen.**

Uniting in Worship, 1988

Sovereign Lord and Father,
through the death and resurrection of your Son
all creation is renewed
and your people are born again:
may we grow up into him
and be brought to fullness of life in Christ;
who is alive and reigns with you and the Holy Spirit,
one God, now and for ever. **Amen.**

An Anglican Prayer Book,
Province of Southern Africa, 1989

The Fifth Sunday of Easter

O Lord and Saviour,
you are the Way, the Truth, and the Life.
Reveal to us your truth
and inspire us with your life,
that now and for ever,
we may find, in you,
the way to God;
and this we ask for your name's sake. **Amen**

H. Bisseker

Assist us, O Lord,
in our proclamation and praise,
that as we exalt the name above all names,
we may enter into the joy of full salvation
and celebrate the eternal victory of your Son,
our Saviour Jesus Christ,
who lives and reigns with you,
in the unity of the Holy Spirit,
now and for ever. **Amen.**

C. N. R. Wallwork

The Sixth Sunday of Easter

God most holy,
in the glorious resurrection of your Son,
our Saviour, Jesus Christ
you have overcome darkness
and restored us to life.
Accept our thanks and praise,
that with your whole church,
on earth and in heaven,
we may extol you and bless your sacred name,
always and everywhere;
through the same Christ our Lord. **Amen.**

C. N. R. Wallwork

From the rising of the sun to its setting,
your name is praised, O Lord,
for you have raised us from the dust
and set before us
the vision of your glory.
As you have bestowed upon us the dignity of a royal priesthood,
lift up our hearts
to celebrate your praise;
through Christ our Lord,
who lives and reigns with you,
and the Holy Spirit;
one God, now and for ever. **Amen**

Celebrating Common Prayer, 1992

Ascension Day

O Christ,
the King of Glory,
who on this day ascended
to the fullness of your eternal kingdom;
assist us with your grace,
that our devotion to your majesty and splendour
may ascend to the throne of your heavenly glory;
where you live and reign,
with the Father, in the unity of the Holy Spirit,
one God, world without end. **Amen.**

C. N. R. Wallwork

Lord Christ,
holy and strong,
holy and immortal:
God from God,
Light from light,
born of a woman,
crucified, risen, ascended;
receive our adoration,
our homage and our love;
now and for ever. **Amen.**

New Every Morning

The Seventh Sunday of Easter
(The Sunday of the Ascension)

Righteous Father,
your beloved Son prayed that his disciples might be one.
Look upon us
gathered in his name,
and fulfil in us the prayer of our Saviour.
Crown our act of praise
with your Spirit's gift of unity and love.
We make our prayer through Jesus Christ,
the firstborn from the dead,
who is alive and reigns with you,
now and always,
in the unity of the Holy Spirit,
one God for ever and ever. **Amen.**

ICEL Collects, 1997

Lord Jesus Christ,
risen from the dead
and gloriously ascended;
bless the prayer and praise
of your faithful people
that prepared and waiting,
we may with your whole church
be clothed with power from on high;
according to your promise,
and for the honour of your holy name. **Amen.**

C. N. R. Wallwork

The Day of Pentecost
(Whit Sunday)

God our Father,
you have promised to give the Holy Spirit
to those who ask you.
Look graciously upon us
assembled with one accord in one place.
As we make our prayer,
and await your promise,
renew our longing hearts
with your holy gift;
through Christ our Lord,
who lives and reigns with you,
in the unity of the Holy Spirit;
one God, now and for ever. **Amen.**

James Ferguson

O God,
we pray that
as the Holy Paraclete came in wind and fire
to the apostles,
so the same Holy Spirit may come to us,
breathing life into our souls
and kindling in our hearts
the flame of love;
through Jesus Christ our Lord. **Amen.**

J. W. G. Masterton

Trinity Sunday
(The Sunday after Pentecost)

O Lord our God,
eternal, immortal and invisible,
the mystery of whose being is unsearchable:
accept our praise
for the revelation of yourself
as Father, Son and Holy Spirit,
three Persons and one God;
and grant that
holding fast to this faith,
we may magnify your glorious name,
for you live and reign, one God,
world without end. **Amen.**

Bishop John Dowden

O God our mystery,
you bring us to life,
call us to freedom,
and move between us with love.
May we so participate
in the dance of your trinity,
that our lives may resonate with you,
now and for ever. **Amen.**

Janet Morley, *All Desires Known*, 1988

Day of Thanksgiving for the Institution of Communion

(The Thursday after Trinity Sunday)
'Corpus Christi'

God our Father,
whose Son at table offered himself as the innocent Lamb,
and gave us this memorial of his passion
until the end of time;
feed your people
and strengthen them in holiness,
that the children of the earth
may live in the light of one faith
in one communion of love;
through the same Christ our Lord. **Amen.**

David Silk, *Prayers for Use at the Alternative Services*, 1980

God our Father,
you refresh your whole church
in this most holy mystery
of our Saviour's body and blood.
May this sacrament of our salvation
turn not to our judgment and condemnation,
but to the strengthening of our souls and bodies
for eternal life;
through Christ our Lord. **Amen.**

Sarum Missal

The Sunday between 24 and 28 May inclusive*

'The Eighth Sunday in Ordinary Time'

* (If after Trinity Sunday)

O Lord our God,
whose glory the Cherubim and Seraphim
and all those hosts of heaven,
with ceaseless voice proclaim:
look upon your servants,
from your dwelling-place,
and in your mercy
accept our prayers and praise;
for the sake of our only Mediator and Advocate,
Jesus Christ our Lord. **Amen.**

*The Book of Common Prayer
of the Scottish Church*, 1912

Grant us, heavenly Father,
reverence, as we proclaim your glory,
understanding, as we recall your compassion,
and gratitude as we praise you for your goodness;
so that we may leave this service
with our knowledge deepened,
our love rekindled
and our lives renewed;
through Jesus Christ our Lord. **Amen.**

Frank Colquhoun, *Contemporary Parish Prayers*, 1975

The Sunday between 29 May and 4 June inclusive*

'The Ninth Sunday in Ordinary Time'

* (If after Trinity Sunday)

Gracious God,
without whose presence all worship is vain,
and without whose light we have no understanding:
lead us into your holy presence,
and bring us from the darkness of our sin
into the brightness of your heavenly light;
that with your whole church,
we may worship you in spirit and in truth,
to the honour of your name,
and the glory of your kingdom,
through Jesus Christ our Lord. **Amen.**

The Book of Common Order, 1928

Gracious God,
reveal yourself this day
in your people's praise,
and inspire our worship
with your Holy Spirit,
that we may know your truth
and bear witness to it in word and deed;
for your name's sake. **Amen.**

C. N. R. Wallwork

The Sunday between 5 and 11 June inclusive*

'The Tenth Sunday in Ordinary Time'

* *(If after Trinity Sunday)*

Gracious God,
whose glory is above all our thoughts
and whose mercy is over all your works;
may your Holy Spirit inspire our worship
and make us attentive to your Word.
Accept, we pray, the sacrifice of praise
which your holy church offers to you this day.
Being created by you,
let us ever act for your glory,
and being redeemed by you,
let us render to you that which is your own;
through Jesus Christ our Lord. **Amen.**

John Wesley, *Collection of Forms of Prayer*, 1733

Open our lips, O Lord,
and purify our hearts,
that we may worthily praise your name.
Help us to be reverent in thought, word and act,
and to worship you at all times
in the faith and spirit
of our Lord and Saviour, Jesus Christ. **Amen.**

John Hunter, *Devotional Services for Public Worship*, 1930

The Sunday between 12 and 18 June inclusive*

'The Eleventh Sunday in Ordinary Time'

* (If after Trinity Sunday)

God of hope,
true light of the faithful
and the perfect brightness of the blessed,
fill our hearts with your Spirit
that we may render you true prayer
and glorify your name for ever,
with the offering of our praise;
through Jesus Christ our Lord. **Amen.**

Gelasian Sacramentary

God of power and love,
pour upon your church today
the gifts of your grace:
that its praise may be strengthened by your Spirit
and its life be enriched by your love;
through Jesus Christ our Lord. **Amen.**

C. N. R. Wallwork

The Sunday between 19 and 25 June inclusive*

'The Twelfth Sunday in Ordinary Time'

* (If after Trinity Sunday)

Keep us, good Lord,
under the shadow of your mercy
and, as you have bound us to yourself in love,
leave us not who call on your name
but grant us your salvation,
made known in Jesus Christ our Lord. **Amen.**

David Stancliffe, *Celebrating Common Prayer*, 1992

God of hope,
fill us with all joy and peace in believing,
that we may serve you with gladness,
delight in doing your will
and rejoice to make melody to you
in our hearts;
through Jesus Christ our Lord. **Amen.**

Frank Colquhoun, *New Parish Prayers*, 1982

The Sunday between 26 June and 2 July inclusive

'The Thirteenth Sunday in Ordinary Time'

O God,
the life of the faithful;
hear the prayers
of those who call upon you,
that in us your promises may be fulfilled
according to the abundance of your mercy;
through Christ our Lord. **Amen.**

Gelasian Sacramentary

Gracious God,
speak to us today
through your Word,
and pour upon us
the gifts of your grace,
that we may learn your will and obey your call;
through Christ our Lord. **Amen.**

F. W. Street, *Prayers for Today's Church*

The Sunday between 3 and 9 July inclusive

'The Fourteenth Sunday in Ordinary Time'

Spirit of the living God,
dwelling in your church
in holiness, wisdom and might;
come and fill the hearts of your people
and kindle in them the fire of your love;
through Jesus Christ our Lord. **Amen.**

Book of Common Order, 1940

Let your Spirit come upon us, O Lord,
that today we may announce good news to the poor;
proclaim release to captives
and recovery of sight to those who cannot see.
Today may the broken victim be set free
and may the coming of the year of jubilee bring justice and peace;
through Christ our Lord. **Amen.**

Prayers for Today's Church

The Sunday between 10 and 16 July inclusive

'The Fifteenth Sunday in Ordinary Time'

Grant, O Lord,
that all who worship within this holy place
may present themselves to you
as a holy, acceptable and living sacrifice.
May we become temples of your holy Spirit
in which you dwell,
now and for ever. **Amen.**

The Book of Worship, 1964

Lord God,
in this act of worship
let us give our minds to you
that we may hear your word.
Let us give our hearts to you,
that we may know what you require of us.
Let us give our strength to you
that through us your will may be done.
This we ask through Jesus Christ our Lord. **Amen.**

Contemporary Prayers for Church and School, 1975

The Sunday between 17 and 23 July inclusive

'The Sixteenth Sunday in Ordinary Time'

Saving God,
in Jesus Christ you have opened for us
a new and living way into your presence:
give us pure hearts and constant wills
to worship you in spirit and in truth;
through the same Jesus Christ our Lord,
who lives and reigns with you and the Holy Spirit,
one God, now and for ever. **Amen.**

A Prayer Book for Australia, 1995

Awaken us to your presence, O God,
that we may bow before you with reverence,
praise you with joy
and serve you with love;
through Jesus Christ our Lord. **Amen.**

J. W. G. Masterton, 1970

The Sunday between 24 and 30 July inclusive

'The Seventeenth Sunday in Ordinary Time'

Bless us, O God,
with a sense of your presence
and with knowledge of your peace,
that we may worship you
with minds alert to your bidding
and with spirits awake to your glory;
through Christ our Lord. **Amen**.

Lutheran Book of Worship, 1979 altered

Grant, O Lord,
that your holy word
may this day be grafted inwardly in our hearts,
that we may both perceive what we ought to do,
and receive the grace and power faithfully to fulfil the same;
and this we ask through Jesus Christ our Lord. **Amen.**

Services for Use in the Diocese of Southwark, 1926

The Sunday between 31 July and 6 August inclusive

'The Eighteenth Sunday in Ordinary Time'

Spirit of God,
glowing and mighty fire,
come and burn in us until your radiance fills our souls,
until your light illumines our minds
and until your love blazes in our hearts;
and this we ask through Christ our Lord. **Amen.**

Chandran Devanesan, 1979

Eternal God,
we come to you, weak and mortal.
Out of your strength and immortality,
reveal to us this day
what we may become in your great purpose.
Lift our eyes beyond the things of time
and our senses to that which is eternal;
through Christ our Lord. **Amen.**

Rita F. Snowden

The Sunday between 7 and 13 August inclusive

'The Nineteenth Sunday in Ordinary Time'

God of grace,
you have given us minds to know you,
hearts to love you,
and voices to sing your praise.
Fill us with your Spirit,
that we may celebrate your glory
and worship you in spirit and in truth;
through Jesus Christ our Lord. **Amen.**

Book of Common Worship, Presbyterian Church USA, 1946

Grant to us, O Lord,
the help of your Holy Spirit,
that, whatever by your teaching we know to be our duty,
we may by your grace be enabled to perform;
through Jesus Christ our Lord. **Amen.**

J. C. Chute, *Daily Prayer*, 1941

The Sunday between 14 and 20 August inclusive

'The Twentieth Sunday in Ordinary Time'

Holy God,
whose majesty is exceeded
only by your love;
grant that our worship
may be penitent in the presence of your holiness,
reverent at the contemplation of your majesty
and confident in the knowledge of your love;
through Jesus Christ our Lord. **Amen.**

C. N. R. Wallwork

Eternal God,
whose only Son, our Saviour,
taught us to worship you in spirit and in truth;
grant us this day
minds enriched by your truth,
and hearts quickened by your spirit.
May we hear your voice
and be eager to accomplish your will;
through the same Christ our Lord. **Amen.**

Prayers for the Christian Year, 1952

The Sunday between 21 and 27 August inclusive

'The Twenty-first Sunday in Ordinary Time'

Lamb of God,
you are worthy to receive
the blessings of all the hosts of heaven.
Shed upon our worship
the bright beams of your everlasting mercy,
that in this, our sacrifice of praise,
we may share the splendour of your eternal kingdom;
for your own name's sake. **Amen.**

C. N. R. Wallwork

O God,
before whose throne
the whole family of heaven and earth
bows down in ceaseless adoration:
accept the praise we offer this day.
May we know the joy of your salvation
that the sorrowing may be comforted,
the faint-hearted be made strong,
and the wayward restored to life and peace;
through Jesus Christ our Lord. **Amen.**

Fred D. Gealey, *The Book of Worship*, 1964

The Sunday between 28 August and 3 September inclusive

'The Twenty-second Sunday in Ordinary Time'

Gracious God,
your glory is the only purpose of our worship.
Accept your people's praise,
inspire our prayers,
and come to us in both word and sacrament;
through Jesus Christ our Lord. **Amen.**

C. N. R. Wallwork

Be near to us, O Lord, in this time of worship.
Open our ears to hear your voice;
our eyes to behold your glory,
our hearts to receive your grace,
and open our mouths to declare your praise;
through Jesus Christ our Lord. **Amen.**

Frank Colquhoun, *Parish Prayers*, 1967

The Sunday between 4 and 10 September inclusive

'The Twenty-third Sunday in Ordinary Time'

Eternal God,
grant to us this day
the gift of your light and grace;
that we see your glory
in the face of our Lord and Saviour, Jesus Christ. **Amen**

C. N. R. Wallwork

God of peace,
you have taught us
that in returning and rest we shall be saved,
and in quietness and confidence is our strength:
By your Holy Spirit,
lift us to your presence
where we may be still
and know that you are God;
through Jesus Christ our Lord. **Amen.**

The Book of Worship, 1964

The Sunday between 11 and 17 September inclusive

'The Twenty-fourth Sunday in Ordinary Time'

Eternal God,
you draw near to us in Christ
and make yourself our guest.
Amid the cares of our daily lives,
make us attentive to your voice
and alert to your presence,
that we may treasure your word above all else;
this we ask through Jesus Christ our Lord. **Amen.**

The Sacramentary, ICEL Collects, 1997

Empower us as we seek your presence, O Lord.
Guide us in our worship,
uphold us till it ends
and grant that our praise
may be to your honour and glory;
through Christ our Lord. **Amen.**

Worship Now, 1972

The Sunday between 18 and 24 September inclusive

'The Twenty-fifth Sunday in Ordinary Time'

Our Father and Lord,
in whom is fullness of light and wisdom;
enlighten our minds by the Holy Spirit
and grant us the grace to receive your word
with reverence and understanding;
through Jesus Christ our Lord. **Amen.**

John Calvin

Father of all,
help us in this act of worship
to celebrate the majesty of your glory,
to proclaim the victory of Christ
and to rejoice in the power of the Holy Spirit;
and this we ask for your love's sake. **Amen.**

C. N. R. Wallwork

The Sunday between 25 September and 1 October inclusive

'The Twenty-sixth Sunday in Ordinary Time'

Gracious God,
make us to be like-minded with all your saints
whether on earth or in heaven.
May we worship you as they worship,
trust you as they trust,
rejoice in you as they rejoice
and love you as they love you;
for the sake of your only Son, our Saviour Jesus Christ. **Amen.**

Christina Rossetti

Eternal God and Father,
cleanse us from all that hinders our communion with you
and with each other.
May our worship be in the fellowship of the Holy Spirit
and in the name of your Son,
Jesus Christ our Lord. **Amen.**

Basil Naylor

The Sunday between 2 and 8 October inclusive

'The Twenty-seventh Sunday in Ordinary Time'

Grant, O merciful God,
that we who confess you with all our mind,
may worship you with all our strength
and love you with all our soul;
and that so confessing, worshipping and loving,
we may behold you at the last in your heavenly glory;
through Jesus Christ our Lord. **Amen.**

Eric Milner-White

Help us, O Lord,
to come before your throne with boldness.
Quicken our conscience,
enlarge our vision
and increase our faith;
through Christ our Lord. **Amen.**

Frank Colquhoun, *Contemporary Parish Prayers*, 1975

The Sunday between 9 and 15 October inclusive

'The Twenty-eighth Sunday in Ordinary Time'

God in whom we live and move and have our being,
help us to worship you in spirit and in truth.
Assured of your love and mercy,
may we come boldly to your throne of grace.
Hungry and thirsty,
may we find your Word meat and drink to our souls.
Eager to know and serve you,
may we see your glory in the face of Jesus Christ our Lord. **Amen.**

R. W. Stewart, 1959

God of glory,
you call us to share in the mystery of worship
with your whole creation
and with all the hosts of heaven.
Grant that adoring you with reverence
and praising you with sincerity
we may offer ourselves to you
in the service of your kingdom;
and this we ask through Jesus Christ our Lord. **Amen.**

Collects with the New Lectionary, 1960

The Sunday between 16 and 22 October inclusive

'The Twenty-ninth Sunday in Ordinary Time'

Eternal God,
as a holy priesthood
may we offer to you this day
a true and spiritual sacrifice.
May our prayers and praise
and the oblation of our lives
be acceptable in your sight;
through Jesus Christ our Lord. **Amen.**

Orders and Prayers for Church Worship, 1960

Gracious God,
help us to be still in your presence,
that we may know ourselves to be your people
and you to be our God;
through Jesus Christ our Lord. **Amen.**

New Every Morning, 1973

The Sunday between 23 and 29 October inclusive

'The Thirtieth Sunday in Ordinary Time'

Gracious God,
through your Holy Spirit
give us grace to sing of your majesty,
and with all creation
to praise and worship you
now and for ever. **Amen.**

Book of Common Worship, 1993

God of the heavens,
God of the earth,
all creation awaits your gift of new life.
Prepare our hearts
to receive the word of your Son,
that his gospel may grow within us
and yield a harvest that is a hundred-fold;
this we ask through Jesus Christ, your Son, our Lord. **Amen**

ICEL Collects, 1997

All Saints' Day (1 November)

or, The Sunday between 30 October and 5 November inclusive

Eternal God,
grant to us that flame of your love
which you kindle
in the hearts of all the saints;
and as we rejoice in their triumphs
so may we profit by their examples;
through Jesus Christ our Lord. **Amen.**

Gothic Missal

Gracious God,
let the light of your glory
appear among us,
that with all your saints
we may be sharers of your eternity;
through Jesus Christ our Lord. **Amen.**

Praise in All Our Days, 1975

The Sunday between 30 October and 5 November inclusive*

'The Thirty-first Sunday in Ordinary Time'

* *(If not observed as All Saints' Day)*

Father of all,
continue, we pray,
your work of love within us,
that as we celebrate the mystery of your salvation
so we may rejoice in your gift of eternal life;
through Christ our Lord. **Amen.**

Pope John XXIII

Lord,
may we who honour the name of Jesus
know his presence in this life
and be filled with the joy of his kingdom
through all eternity;
where he lives and reigns with you,
for ever and ever. **Amen.**

From a fifteenth-century litany

The Sunday between 6 and 12 November inclusive

'The Thirty-second Sunday in Ordinary Time'

Holy Spirit,
as we gather in your name,
enlighten our hearts,
reveal your will
and guide us with your wisdom
that we may be united to you
with bonds of love, faithful and true;
through Christ our Lord. **Amen.**

Isidore of Seville, *c.* 560–636

God of all grace,
increase in us today
the love of your name,
sensitivity to your word
and peace and joy in the Holy Spirit;
through Christ our Lord. **Amen.**

C. N. R. Wallwork

The Sunday between 13 and 19 November inclusive

'The Thirty-third Sunday in Ordinary Time'

Lord our God,
in this time of worship,
make your presence known to us.
Purify our hearts that we may see you,
inspire our minds that we may love you
and cleanse our souls that we may come to you;
through Christ our Lord. **Amen.**

C. N. R. Wallwork

Come, Holy Spirit,
restore the lives which, without you,
are lifeless and dead.
Kindle the hearts which, without you,
are cold and dull.
Enlighten the minds which, without you,
are dark and blind.
Fill the church which, without you,
is an empty shrine;
and enfold your people in your divine glory;
through Christ our Lord. **Amen.**

New Every Morning, 1973

The Sunday between 20 and 26 November inclusive

The Sunday before Advent
'Feast of Christ the King'

Almighty God,
may your glory fill our worship
as we proclaim your Son
King of kings, and Lord of lords;
and accept the homage of your people
as we offer our lives in the service
of your eternal kingdom;
now and for ever. **Amen.**

Book of Common Worship, 1993

Gracious God,
you have anointed your Son, our Saviour,
a king and priest for ever.
Show us in his death
the victory that crowns the ages
and in his broken body
the love that unites heaven and earth;
and this we ask for Jesus' sake. **Amen.**

ICEL Collects, 1997

Part Two

Prayers for Special Occasions

Feasts of Apostles

Inspire our zeal, O Lord,
and quicken our devotion,
that in the glorious company of *N.*,
and all your apostles,
we may offer to you
mouths to proclaim your praise
and lives dedicated to your service;
through Jesus Christ our Lord. **Amen.**

C. N. R. Wallwork

Bind us in fellowship, O Lord,
with *N.*, and all your apostles,
that we may offer you the praise
of glad and thankful hearts;
and grant that having confessed your name on earth
we may rejoice to behold your glory in heaven;
through Jesus Christ our Lord. **Amen.**

C. N. R. Wallwork

Feasts of Martyrs

Grant us, O Christ,
a share in the blood of the martyrs
which is the seed of your church;
and unite us with *N.*,
and all who are witnesses to your grace,
that our praise may mingle with theirs
before the throne of your glory;
for you live and reign, now and for ever. **Amen.**

C. N. R. Wallwork

Inspire our worship, O Lord,
with the memory of *N.*,
and all your martyrs,
whom we celebrate today.
May the example of their faithfulness give us courage
to proclaim the message of your Cross in word and deed;
through Christ our Lord. **Amen.**

Lutheran Book of Worship, 1979

Feasts of Saints

Almighty God,
in every generation
your church is enriched
through the love and devotion of your saints.
Bless our worship today,
and grant that we who rejoice
in the fellowship of your servant *N.*,
may behold at last the perfect vision of your glory;
through Jesus Christ our Lord. **Amen.**

The Alternative Service Book, 1980 altered

Fill our hearts with gratitude, O God,
as we commemorate your servant *N.*,
and grant that in this our sacrifice of praise
we may rejoice in the presence of all your saints.
Inspired by their fellowship
may the devotion of your church on earth
become one with the worship of heaven;
through Jesus Christ our Lord. **Amen.**

C. N. R. Wallwork

Feasts of Missionaries

Gracious God,
we give you thanks for the mission of your kingdom
and for all who have had a share in it.
As we rejoice in the gifts of *N.*,
whose life we remember today,
receive our praise,
accept our devotion
and renew our life with yours;
through Christ our Lord. **Amen.**

C. N. R. Wallwork

Eternal God,
whose servants *N.* & *N.* shared the good news of your Son
by their whole-hearted sacrifice;
grant that we who give thanks for them today,
may be led through our worship
to offer ourselves in your service;
through Christ our Lord. **Amen.**

C. N. R. Wallwork

Feasts of The Blessed Virgin Mary

Almighty God,
grant that through the merits of your Son,
our Saviour Jesus Christ,
we may offer you true and faithful worship
and in the company of Mary his mother,
come with all your saints
to our everlasting rest;
through the same Christ our Lord. **Amen.**

C. N. R. Wallwork

O Christ and God incarnate,
whose Virgin Mother
was blessed in bearing you,
and still more blessed in keeping your word;
grant that we who honour her lowliness
may follow the example of her devotion
until at length we rejoice before you
with all the saints in light;
for ever and ever. **Amen**

William Bright, *Ancient Collects*, 1861

Feasts of John the Baptist

Gracious God, in every age
you raise up prophets like John the Baptist.
As we give thanks this day
for the example of his life,
may the urgency of his preaching
and the courage of his ministry
make us ready to receive the One he announced,
even your Son, our Saviour, Jesus Christ. **Amen.**

ICEL Collects, 1997

Father and Judge of all,
as we rejoice this day
in the ministry of John the Baptist,
help us to accept at your hands,
judgment for our sins
and forgiveness for our penitence;
and this we ask for the sake of your Son,
Jesus Christ our Lord. **Amen.**

C. N. R. Wallwork

Conversion of Saint Paul

God of all grace,
as we celebrate today
the conversion of your Apostle Paul,
grant that may we turn to the light of Christ
and receive your commission
to proclaim the gospel to all nations;
through Jesus Christ our Lord. **Amen.**

C. N. R. Wallwork

Redeeming God,
open our hearts this day
to your loving purposes.
As we give thanks for the message and mission of Paul
we may be crucified with Christ
and through the gifts of your grace
be brought to the glory of your new creation,
where you live and reign for ever and ever. **Amen.**

C. N. R. Wallwork

Church Anniversary, or Feast of Dedication

Let your presence
fill this house of prayer, O Lord,
and grant that all who worship you here,
may be numbered at last
with those who sing your praise
before the throne of your heavenly glory;
through Christ our Lord. **Amen.**

Frank Colquhoun, *Parish Prayers*, 1967

Father,
each year we recall the dedication of this church
to your service.
Let all our worship be sincere
and here may we find your saving love.
Grant this through Jesus Christ, your Son,
who lives and reigns with you and the Holy Spirit,
one God, for ever and ever. **Amen.**

The Sunday Missal, 1975

Annual Covenant Service

Merciful God,
accept the worship of your people this day.
Grant that with contrite hearts
and solemn vow
we may renew the covenant
which in every generation
binds a faithful people
to a loving God;
and this we ask through Jesus Christ our Lord. **Amen.**

C. N. R. Wallwork

God of peace,
you call men and women to repentance,
and in your grace
you have met their needs in a new covenant.
Grant us penitence for our sin,
enable us to fulfil the ministry you set before us
and make us holy in every part of our being;
through Christ out Lord. **Amen.**

Collects with the New Lectionary, 1972

Conversions of John and Charles Wesley

Almighty God,
out of your free and universal grace
we receive both the assurance of faith
and the holiness of perfect love.
Bless our ministry of praise
and the proclamation of your gospel
that we may rejoice once more
as pardoned sinners made welcome in your kingdom;
through Jesus Christ our Lord. **Amen.**

C. N. R. Wallwork

In your goodness, O Lord,
you assure us of your love and grace.
Grant that in this hour of worship
sins may be forgiven,
hope rekindled
and power bestowed,
that our lives may reflect your honour and glory;
through Jesus Christ our Lord. **Amen**

Church of Scotland, *The Divine Service*, 1973

Harvest Thanksgiving

Gracious God,
you have given us the fruits of the earth
in their seasons,
and crowned the year with your goodness.
Give us grateful hearts,
that we may thank you for your loving kindness
and worthily offer our praise to your holy name;
through Jesus Christ our Lord. **Amen.**

Bishop John Dowden

Lord,
whose mercy reaches to the heavens
and whose faithfulness knows no end,
let the greatness of your love
be known to us,
that we may worship you
with wonder, joy and thanksgiving;
through Jesus Christ our Lord. **Amen**

New Every Morning, 1973

World Church Sunday

Eternal Father,
from whom every family in heaven and earth is named,
unite us, as we worship you here,
with all who in far-off places
are lifting up their hands and hearts to you.
May your church throughout the world,
with the church in heaven,
offer up one sacrifice of thanksgiving,
to the praise and honour of your holy name;
through Christ our Lord. **Amen.**

Eric Milner-White and G. W. Briggs

Send forth your Spirit, O Lord,
and renew the face of the earth.
May the light of your gospel
bring life to the nations
and may the praise of your whole church
resound for ever to the glory of your name;
through Jesus Christ our Lord. **Amen**

C. N. R. Wallwork

Social Responsibility Sunday

Go with us, Lord,
into your holy place.
Guide our worship
and bless your word.
Save us from hypocrisy,
and deliver us from evil;
for the sake of your Son,
our Saviour Jesus Christ. **Amen**

Book of Common Order, 1940

Eternal Light,
lead us into your presence,
speak to our hearts
and bring us into the glorious liberty
of the children of God;
and this we ask through Christ our Lord. **Amen.**

Contemporary Prayers for Church and School, 1975

A Remembrance Sunday Service

God, our Refuge and our Strength,
by whose mercy and providence we are protected
and by whose love we are redeemed,
grant us the help of your Holy Spirit
that we may praise you for your goodness
and offer you true and acceptable worship;
through Jesus Christ our Lord. **Amen.**

James M. Todd

Eternal Son of the Father,
who for our salvation became one with us
in everything except sin,
grant us the light of your liberating word,
that hearing it
we may act upon it
and be led thereby into your kingdom
where you live and reign for ever. **Amen.**

Praise in All Our Days, 1975

New Year or Annual Watchnight Service

Gracious God,
we have heard you call us by name
and we have come to offer you our praise,
and to hear your most holy word.
Be present in our midst
that this may be for us an hour of light,
in which we see heaven opened,
and the brightness of your glory upon this dark earth;
and this we ask through Christ our Lord. **Amen.**

Karl Barth

Lord Jesus,
you asked your disciples to watch with you
for one brief hour of prayer.
Bless our midnight songs of praise,
that in these solemn moments
we may know your presence
and be awake to your glory;
through Christ our Lord. **Amen.**

C. N. R. Wallwork

Octave of Prayer for Christian Unity

In this your house, O Lord,
may we dwell in peace and concord
with one heart and mind
and one true interpretation of your holy word.
May the one body of Christ
be filled with the one Spirit
and extol your holy name together;
through Jesus Christ our Lord. **Amen.**

Godly Prayers, 1552

Lord our God,
Giver of all grace,
have mercy on your whole church.
Renew its life,
restore its unity
and sanctify its worship.
Through your power
may we become an instrument
fit for your purposes
and dedicated to the life of your kingdom;
through Jesus Christ our Lord. **Amen.**

Frank Colquhoun

Commissioning of Preachers and Readers

Almighty God,
grant us the gift of your grace,
that the prayers which are offered to you
and the vows which are made before you
may be a blessing to your church and people;
through Jesus Christ our Lord. **Amen**

C. N. R. Wallwork

Lord our God,
you have taught us in the scriptures
that the people shall not hear
without a preacher.
Therefore we pray you to pour out your Spirit
on the worship of your church today
that each of your servants may remain faithful in their
vocation and ministry;
and this we ask through Jesus Christ our Lord. **Amen.**

C. N. R. Wallwork

Recognition or Commissioning of an Authorized Lay Ministry

Gracious God,
your Son, our Saviour Jesus Christ,
came among us not to be served but to serve.
Grant that as we seek your Holy Spirit
in this hour of dedication
so we may be ready
to spend and be spent in your service;
through the same Christ our Lord. **Amen**

C. N. R. Wallwork

Into your hands, O Lord,
we commend this our worship of you,
and this our time of vow and dedication.
May your Spirit rest upon all who look to you today
for guidance and blessing;
and this we ask through Christ our Lord. **Amen.**

C. N. R. Wallwork

Commissioning of Pastoral Leaders

God our Father,
you provide for your people with tenderness
and you rule over them in love.
In this our act of praise
may we worship you aright
and through the gifts of your Spirit
may your servants be equipped
for their ministry and service;
and this we ask through Jesus Christ our Lord. **Amen.**

Gregorian Sacramentary

God our Shepherd,
grant to your church and people
pastoral leaders after your own heart;
and pour out on us today
the inspiration and blessing of the Holy Spirit;
through Jesus Christ our Lord,
who lives and reigns
with you and the Holy Spirit,
now and for ever. **Amen.**

C. N. R. Wallwork

At a Baptism or Confirmation

God our Father,
accept those for whom the church prays today
and grant to us all
the forgiveness of our sins
and the gifts of your Holy Spirit;
through Jesus Christ our Lord. **Amen.**

C. N. R. Wallwork

God of all grace,
whose beloved Son
promised the Comforter
to his disciples,
pour out your Spirit on your people today
that they may rejoice
in your new creation
and be brought to fullness of life,
through Jesus Christ our Lord. **Amen**

C. N. R. Wallwork

A Welcome or Induction Service

Faithful God,
in every age you bless your people
with the pastors and teachers of your own choice;
bless your church and servants today,
and inspire our sacrifice of praise,
with the gifts of your Holy Spirit;
through Jesus Christ our Lord. **Amen.**

C. N. R. Wallwork

God our Father,
we give you thanks and praise
for those whom Christ has called
to shepherd and guide your flock.
Bless the worship which we offer to you now,
and unite your church and people
in the service and joy of your kingdom;
and this we ask through Jesus Christ our Lord. **Amen.**

C. N. R. Wallwork

A Choral Festival or Songs of Praise

Lord our God,
whose glory all the hosts of heaven
with ceaseless voice proclaim;
accept, we pray, the praise of your church below,
and pour out upon us
that spirit of reverence and joy
which shall lift both our hymns and our lives to you;
through Jesus Christ our Lord. **Amen.**

Eric Milner-White

Bless, O God,
those who with hymns, and psalms and spiritual songs
make melody in their hearts to you.
May their anthems of praise be one
with the songs of the saints in light;
through Jesus Christ our Lord. **Amen.**

C. N. R. Wallwork

Acknowledgements

The Compiler wishes to express his thanks to the following for permission to reproduce prayers of which they are the authors, publishers or copyright holders. In a few instances it has not been possible to trace ownership. If there has been any infringement of copyright it is hoped that this will be pardoned.

James Clark & Co. Ltd for prayers from *Prayers for Common Worship* by James Ferguson (originally published by Allenson & Co. Ltd)

Material from *Celebrating Common Prayer* (Mowbray), © The Society of Saint Francis 1992, is used with permission

Abingdon Press, Nashville, USA for a prayer from *The Book of Worship* (1945), for prayers from *The Book of Worship* (1964) and for a prayer from *The United Methodist Book of Worship* (1992)

International Commission on English in the Liturgy, Inc. for collects from *The Sacramentary, Volume One: Sundays and Feasts* © 1997 and for the English translation of a prayer from the *Roman Missal*, Copyright © 1973

A. R. Mowbray & Co. Ltd for prayers from *After the Third Collect* by Eric Milner-White and from *Prayers for use at the Alternative Services* by David Silk

Geoffrey Chapman Publishers for a prayer from *A Christian's Prayer Book* by Peter Coughlan, Ronald C. D. Jasper and Teresa Rodrigues

The Anglican Church of Canada for three collects from *The Book of Alternative Services of the Anglican Church of Canada* (1985)

The Friends of York Minster for a prayer from *A Procession of Passion Prayers* by Eric Milner-White and for a prayer from *A Cambridge Bede Book* also by Eric Milner-White

The Church Hymnal Corporation, New York for three prayers from *The Book of Common Prayer: The Episcopal Church USA* (1977)

The Church of the Province of New Zealand for the use of four prayers from *A New Zealand Prayer Book* (1989)

The Church Pastoral Aid Society for two prayers from *Prayers for Today's Church* edited by R. H. C. Williams (1972)

Hodder & Stoughton Ltd. for prayers from three books edited by Canon Frank Colquhoun, *Parish Prayers* (1967), *Contemporary Parish Prayers* (1975) and *New Parish Prayers* (1982)

The Provincial Trustees of the Church of the Province of South Africa for a collect from *An Anglican Prayer Book* 1989

The Uniting Church in Australia for three prayers from *Uniting in Worship* (1988)

The General Synod of the Scottish Episcopal Church for two collects from *The Scottish Book of Common Prayer* (1929) and a collect from *The Book of Common Prayer of the Scottish Church* (1912)

Broughton Books, E. J. Dwyer (Australia) Pty. Ltd. for two prayers from *A Prayer Book for Australia* (1995)

Augsburg Publishing House, USA for two prayers from the *Lutheran Book of Worship* (1979)

The Baptist Union for a prayer from *Orders and Prayers for Church Worship* edited by Ernest Payne and Stephen Winward (1960)

Janet Morley for two prayers from *All Desires Known* published by The Movement for the Ordination of Women (1988)

SCM Press for a prayer from *A Book of Prayers for Schools* edited by Hugh Martin (1936) and two prayers from *Contemporary Prayers for Church and School* edited by Caryl Micklem (1975)

SPCK for a prayer by Michael Perham in *Enriching the Christian Year* (1993) and for a prayer in *Services for Use in the Diocese of Southwark* (1926)

Grove Books Ltd. for three prayers from *Collects with the New Lectionary* by Akehurst and Bishop (1972 and 1973)

The World Church Office of the Methodist Church in Great Britain and Ireland for a prayer by Chandran Devanesan from *The World Calls Christians to Prayer*

The Liturgical Press Collegeville, USA for a prayer from *Pray Without Ceasing* (1993)

The Society of the Faith and Church Union Trustees (Incorporated) for an English translation of a prayer from *Praise in All our Days: Common Prayer at Taizé* (1975)

The United Reformed Church for two prayers from *A Book of Services and Prayers* (1959) published by The Independent Press

The Epworth Press for a prayer from *Selected Prayers by Karl Barth* (1966)

The BBC for prayers from *New Every Morning* (New Edition 1973) edited by James M. Todd

Westminster John Knox Press, Louisville, USA for a prayer from the

1946 *Book of Common Worship* and for two prayers from the *Book of Common Worship* © (1993)

Edward Francis Gabriele for a collect from *Prayers for Dawn and Dusk* published by St Mary's Press, Winona, USA (1992)

The Church of Scotland Panel on Worship for a prayer from *Prayers for Use in Church* by J. W. G. Masterton (1970), for a prayer from *Worship Now* edited by David Cairns (1972), prayers from *The Book of Common Order* (1940), a prayer from *Prayers for the Christian Year* (1952) and a prayer from *The Divine Service* (1973)

Oxford University Press for prayers from *Daily Prayer* edited by G. W. Briggs and Eric Milner-White (1941)

The Church of England: Church House Publishing for a prayer from *The Alternative Service Book* (1980), for a prayer from *Lent, Holy Week and Easter* (1984) and a prayer from *Common Worship Initiation Services* (1998)

The Uniting Presbyterian Church in Southern Africa for a prayer from the *Service Book and Ordinal* (1969) published by the Presbyterian Church of South Africa

Sources of Prayers

1 The source in the left-hand column refers to the first prayer on each page and that in the right-hand column to the second.

2 The figures after each code refer to the page number in that particular book.

Sundays of Advent

1st	BWW	ADK 9
2nd	NJP	UW 147
3rd	ICEL 6	CNL 35
4th	MM	CPB 335

Christmas Eve

	UW 151	CO 653
	BWW	BWW

Christmas Day

	LS	CPB 70

Christmas 1

	ICEL 13	BASC 276

Christmas 2

	NZ 642	PDD 53

Epiphany

	PPP 3	CPP 29

Epiphany 1

	CWIS 49	CPB 84

Sundays in Ordinary Time

2nd	BCPEC 215	NPP 200
3rd	NZ 564	DP 25
4th	PCG 83	BWW

Presentation of Christ

	ICEL 127	PWC 466

Sundays in Ordinary Time

5th	JB	BWW
6th	BW 169	NEM 118
7th	CCP 651	SBO 134
8th	BWW	BWW

The Sunday before Lent

	PWC 352	NEM 5

Ash Wednesday

	BASC 286	ECR 6

Sundays in Lent

1st	SCWH 39	BWW
2nd	BCWW 247	BCO 48
3rd	PBA 487	BVP 45
4th	LHWE 51	BWW
5th	BVP 45	BVP 43
6th	BCO 242	BVP 46

Holy Week

	NZ 583	BASC 302

Maundy Thursday

	DS 148	BWW

Good Friday
    NPP 55   PPP 4

Holy Saturday
    BCPEC 221 BOS 72

Easter Vigil
    NZ 591   UMBW 371

Easter Day
    CPP 57   NEM 34

Sundays of Easter

2nd	GS	BVP 50
3rd	MM	BWW
4th	UW 189	APB 236
5th	BPS 274	BWW
6th	BWW	CCP 634

Ascension Day
    BVP 56   NEM 21

Sundays of Easter

7th	ICEL 49	BWW

The Day of Pentecost
    PCW 203   PUC 77

Trinity Sunday
    SBCP 349   ADK 19

Corpus Christi
    PAS 9   BAC 157

Sundays in Ordinary Time

8th	BCPS 52	CPP 108
9th	FCO 193	BWW
10th	JW	DSH 51
11th	BAC 4	BWW
12th	CCP 607	NPP 256
13th	BAC 4	PTC No.429
14th	BCO 73	PTC No.130

15th	BW 170	CPCS 11
16th	PBA 487	PUC 45
17th	LBW 47	SS 48
18th	CD	RS
19th	BCWW 18	DP 55
20th	BVP 71	PCR 63
21st	BVP 72	BW 167
22nd	BVP 73	PP 351
23rd	BWW	BW 166
24th	ICEL 87	WN 185
25th	JC	BVP 77
26th	DP 115	CPP 106
27th	CB 9	CPP 105
28th	BSP 128	CNL 29
29th	OP 62	NEM 93
30th	BCWW 783	ICEL 84

All Saints' Day
    GM   PAD 309

Sundays in Ordinary Time

31st	PJ	BWW
32nd	BWW	BWW
33rd	BWW	NEM 55

The Sunday before Advent
    BWW   ICEL 123

Feasts of Apostles
    BCW   BWW

Feasts of Martyrs
    BWW   LBW 37

Feasts of Saints
    ASB 871   BWW

Feasts of Missionaries
    BWW   BWW

Feasts of The Blessed Virgin Mary
    BWW   BAC 236

Feasts of John the Baptist
ICEL 130   BWW

Conversion of Saint Paul
BWW   BWW

Church Anniversary,
or Feast of Dedication
PP 177   SM 777

Annual Covenant Service
BWW   CNL 29

Conversions of John and
Charles Wesley
BVP 88   TDS 30

Harvest Thanksgiving
SBCP 293   NEM 13

World Church Sunday
DP 68   BWW

Social Responsibility Sunday
BCO 3   CPCS 9

A Remembrance Sunday Service
BSP 228   PAD 235

New Year or Watchnight
SPB 60   BVP 94

Octave of Prayer for Christian
Unity
DP 111   CPP 174

Commissioning of Preachers
and Readers
BWW   BWW

Recognition or Commissioning
of an Authorized Lay Ministry
BWW   BWW

Commissioning of Pastoral
Leaders
GRS   BWW

At a Baptism or Confirmation
BWW   BWW

A Welcome or Induction Service
BWW   BWW

A Choral Festival or Songs of
Praise
ATC 35   BWW

Code to Sources of Prayers

ADK   ALL DESIRES KNOWN, Janet Morley, MOW 1988

APB   AN ANGLICAN PRAYER BOOK, Church of the Province of South Africa, Collins Liturgical Publications 1989

ASB   THE ALTERNATIVE SERVICE BOOK 1980, The Central Board of Finance of the Church of England

ATC   AFTER THE THIRD COLLECT, Eric Milner-White, Mowbray 1952

BAC   ANCIENT COLLECTS, William Bright, James Parker & Co 1902

BASC   THE BOOK OF ALTERNATIVE SERVICES OF THE ANGLICAN CHURCH OF CANADA, Anglican Book Centre, Toronto 1985

BCO   BOOK OF COMMON ORDER, Church of Scotland, Oxford 1940

BCPEC   THE BOOK OF COMMON PRAYER: THE EPISCOPAL CHURCH USA, The Seabury Press 1977

BCPS   THE BOOK OF COMMON PRAYER OF THE SCOTTISH CHURCH, 1912

BCW   BOOK OF COMMON WORSHIP, Presbyterian Church USA 1946

BCWW   BOOK OF COMMON WORSHIP, Presbyterian Church USA, John Knox Press 1993

BOS   THE BOOK OF OCCASIONAL SERVICES, New York 1994

BPS   A BOOK OF PRAYERS FOR SCHOOLS, SCM Press 1936

BSP   A BOOK OF SERVICES AND PRAYERS, Independent Press Ltd. 1959

BVP   A BOOK OF VESTRY PRAYERS, C. N. R. Wallwork, Epworth Press 1976

BW   THE BOOK OF WORSHIP, The United Methodist Church Nashville 1964, 1965

BWW	BEFORE WE WORSHIP, Norman Wallwork, Epworth Press 2001
CB	A CAMBRIDGE BEDE BOOK, Eric Milner-White, Longman, Green & Co. 1936
CCP	CELEBRATING COMMON PRAYER, Society of Saint Francis 1992
CNL	COLLECTS WITH THE NEW LECTIONARY, Akehurst and Bishop, Grove Books 1972, 1973
CO	BOOK OF COMMON ORDER, Saint Andrew Press 1994
CPB	A CHRISTIAN'S PRAYER BOOK, Peter Coughlan, Ronald Jasper and Teresa Rodrigues, Geoffrey Chapman 1973
CPCS	CONTEMPORARY PRAYERS FOR CHURCH AND SCHOOL, ed. Caryl Micklem, SCM Press 1975
CPP	CONTEMPORARY PARISH PRAYERS, Frank Colquhoun, Hodder & Stoughton 1975
CWIS	COMMON WORSHIP: INITIATION SERVICES, Church Publishing House 1998
DP	DAILY PRAYER, eds. G. W. Briggs and E. Milner-White, Oxford 1941
DS	DIVINE SERVICE, W. E. Orchard, Oxford University Press 1919
DSH	DEVOTIONAL SERVICES FOR PUBLIC WORHIP, John Hunter, J. M. Dent & Sons Ltd. 1930
ECR	ENRICHING THE CHRISTIAN YEAR, SPCK/Alcuin Club 1993
FCO	BOOK OF COMMON ORDER 1928, Oxford University Press
GS	GELASIAN SACRAMENTARY
GRS	GREGORIAN SACRAMENTARY
HI	HIS INTERPRETERS, Rita Snowden, Epworth
ICEL	OPENING PRAYERS, The 1997 ICEL Collects, Canterbury Press 1999
IS	Isidore of Seville
JB	Jacob Boehme
LBW	LUTHERAN BOOK OF WORSHIP, Augsburg Publishing House 1979

LHWE	LENT, HOLY WEEK AND EASTER, Church House Publishing 1984
LS	LEONINE SACRAMENTARY
MM	MOZARABIC MISSAL
MR	MESSALE ROMANO 1983
NEM	NEW EVERY MORNING, New Edition BBC London 1973
NJP	NON-JURORS PRAYER BOOK 1734
NPP	NEW PARISH PRAYERS, Frank Colquhoun, Hodder and Stoughton 1982
NZ	A NEW ZEALAND PRAYER BOOK, Collins 1989
OP	ORDERS AND PRAYERS FOR CHURCH WORSHIP, Ernest A. Payne and Stephen F. Winward, Baptist Union 1960, 1965
PAD	PRAISE IN ALL OUR DAYS, Common Prayer at Taizé, Faith Press 1975
PAS	PRAYERS FOR USE AT THE ALTERNATIVE SERVICES, David Silk, Mowbrays 1980
PBA	A PRAYER BOOK FOR AUSTRALIA, Broughton Books 1995
PCG	PRAYERS FOR THE CITY OF GOD, G. C. Binyon, Longmans 1915
PCR	PRAYERS FOR THE CHRISTIAN YEAR, Saint Andrew Press 1952
PCW	PRAYERS FOR COMMON WORSHIP, James Ferguson, Allenson 1936
PDD	PRAYERS FOR DAWN AND DUSK, Edward F. Gabriele, St Mary's Press, Minnesota 1992
PJ	Pope John XXIII
PP	PARISH PRAYERS, Frank Colquhoun, Hodder & Stoughton 1967
PPP	A PROCESSION OF PASSION PRAYERS, Eric Milner-White, SPCK 1950
PSB	PRESBYTERIAN SERVICE BOOK, Presbyterian Church of England 1968
PTC	PRAYERS FOR TODAY'S CHURCH, CPAS Publications London 1970

PUC	PRAYERS FOR USE IN CHURCH, J. W. G. Masterton, Saint Andrew Press 1970
PWC	PRAY WITHOUT CEASING, Liturgical Press, Minnesota 1993
SBCP	THE SCOTTISH BOOK OF COMMON PRAYER, Edinburgh, Cambridge University Press 1929
SBO	SERVICE BOOK AND ORDINAL, Presbyterian Church of South Africa 1969
SCWH	SUNDAY CELEBRATION OF THE WORD AND HOURS, National Liturgical Office, Canada 1995
SM	THE SUNDAY MISSAL, Collins 1975
SPB	SELECTED PRAYERS, Karl Barth, Epworth Press 1966
SS	SERVICES FOR USE IN THE DIOCESE OF SOUTHWARK, SPCK 1926
TDS	THE DIVINE SERVICE Church of Scotland, Oxford University Press 1973
UMBW	THE UNITED METHODIST BOOK OF WORSHIP, The United Methodist Publishing House, Nashville, Tennessee 1992
UW	UNITING IN WORSHIP, Uniting Church Press, Melbourne 1988
WCCP	THE WORLD CALLS CHRISTIANS TO PRAYER, Cargate Press 1979
WN	WORSHIP NOW, ed. David Cairns, Saint Andrew Press 1972